CULTURE ENCYCLOPEDIA

MUSIC

CULTURE ENCYCLOPEDIA

MUSIC

Antony Mason

Miles Kelly PUBLISHING

First published in 2002 by
Miles Kelly Publishing Ltd
The Bardfield Centre
Great Bardfield
Essex CM7 4SL

© Miles Kelly Publishing 2002

2 4 6 8 10 9 7 5 3 1

Author
Antony Mason

Designed and Edited by
Starry Dog Books

Project Editor
Belinda Gallagher

Assistant Editors
Mark Darling, Nicola Jessop, Isla Macuish

Artwork Commissioning
Lesley Cartlidge

Indexer
Jane Parker

Picture Research
Ruth Boardman, Liberty Newton

Colour Reproduction
DPI Colour, Saffron Walden, Essex

ISBN 1-84236-227-5

Printed in China

A British Library Cataloguing-in-Publication Data
A catalogue record for this book is available from the British Library

www.mileskelly.net
info@mileskelly.net

Contents

INTRODUCTION 6

MAKING MUSIC 8

PERCUSSION INSTRUMENTS 10

WIND INSTRUMENTS 12

STRINGED INSTRUMENTS 14

KEYBOARD INSTRUMENTS 16

HYBRID INSTRUMENTS 18

VOICE 20

PLAYING TOGETHER 22

COMPOSERS 24

CLASSICAL MUSIC 26

IMPROVISATION 28

RECORDED MUSIC 30

THE MUSIC INDUSTRY 32

WORLD MUSIC 34

GLOSSARY 36

INDEX 38

ACKNOWLEDGEMENTS 40

Music

MUSIC is the most popular and widespread of all the arts. We whistle, hum and sing; we listen to music on the radio, on CD players. Many people learn to play musical instruments. Every nation and culture in the world has its own traditions of music. In the Western world, music developed into a highly complex art, involving orchestras of more than a hundred players. Fashions in music change all the time, and with them the instruments used to play it. These days, computers and electronic equipment can produce almost any kind of sound, and the most popular music in the world is often made by just a few musicians and singers. But the effect is similar: music appeals to our ears and emotions. It soothes or excites. It sets our imaginations alight.

Making music

MUSIC is the oldest of all the art forms. The very earliest humans discovered that certain objects – hollow tree trunks, different kinds of stone and the bones of large animals, for example – made curious ringing sounds when struck. A set of decorated mammoth bones found in a hut in Mezin, in the Ukraine, appears to have been used as musical instruments – a 20,000 year-old orchestra! Over time, the range of instruments increased. People jangled small bones as rattles; made drums from animal skins; and blew into hollow bamboo and bones to produce notes. Gradually these instruments were refined and standardized, and the skills needed to play them were taught to others.

◢ TAMBOURINE

A tambourine is a simple kind of drum made of animal skin stretched over a wooden frame. Metal disks inserted into gaps in the frame jangle when the tambourine is shaken. Tambourines were played in ancient Egypt, and were brought to Europe in medieval times during the Crusades.

◄ NAZCA DRUM

About 2000 years ago, the Nazca people of Peru in South America made elaborately painted pottery drums. It is thought that these were played during religious ceremonies. Such ceremonies may have been held on the site of the famous Nazca lines – vast patterns (many depicting animals) made from pathways marked out in the desert.

◄ STRINGED INSTRUMENTS

More than 4000 years ago, the ancient Egyptians played harps – called bow harps because of their shape – to accompany singers at funeral ceremonies. Pictures of them have been found on tomb walls. Harps and other instruments also formed small 'dance bands'.

THE FIRST INSTRUMENT

The oldest instrument of all is the human voice. From the beginning of human existence, human beings made calls to communicate (as do many other living creatures). As they developed their vocal cords for speech, no doubt they also began to explore the creative possibilities of sound by singing, perhaps accompanied by rhythmic clapping.

◨ DIDGERIDOO

The culture of the Australian Aborigines dates back some 50,000 years. The Aborigines most famous musical instrument is the didgeridoo. Traditional didgeridoos are made from tree trunks that have been hollowed out by termites. The deep droning sound is played to accompany singing and dancing.

◸ MAYAN WHISTLE

The Mayan civilization of Mexico and Central America, with its cities and soaring temple-pyramids, reached its peak between AD 600 and 900. This Mayan pottery whistle dates from this period. As with many early instruments, the maker has had fun by creating it in the form of a sculpture.

◪ PANPIPES

Ancient peoples discovered that tubes of different lengths produce different sounds when blown. Panpipes are made of a row of tubes bound together, each cut to a precise length to produce a specific note. The instrument is played by blowing across the tops of the tubes. Panpipes are named after the Greek god Pan, who is said to have made the first musical instrument from a reed.

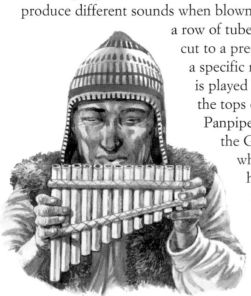

Percussion instruments

INSTRUMENTS that are struck are known as
percussion instruments, from the Latin word
percutere, meaning to hit'. After the human voice, they
are the world's most ancient kind of instrument. The
sound made by some percussion instruments – such as
cymbals, xylophones and bells – comes from the ringing
sound of the material from which they are made. Drums,
on the other hand, have a sound box that amplifies, or
increases, the sound made when the skin, or membrane,
of the 'drumhead' is struck. Drums are used to beat out
rhythms, but they can also be finely tuned to produce
precise notes. The steel drums of Trinidad, for example,
are made from empty oil drums and have
carefully indented, dish-shaped tops
that produce a scale of notes.

◤ AZTEC DRUM

During the 15th century, the Aztecs of Mexico
made a drum called a *teponatzli* from a hollow
log with a slot at the top. It was played with
rubber-tipped drumsticks. Log drums give off
a ringing sound that resonates around the
empty space inside the log.

◧ SHINTO TEMPLE DRUM

Giant drums, accompanied by gongs and
flutes, are used in the temple ceremonies of
Japan's oldest religion, Shinto.
The drums, called *wadaiko*,
are still being made today.
The largest one ever made
was built in 1996. Made of
wood and leather, its
drumheads measure
1.8 metres across and
it weighs 4 tons. In
the past, temple
drums also acted
as warning
sirens.

◧ AFRICAN DRUMS

Drums play a central role in African
music, as this dancing troupe from
Gambia indicates. A drummer can
produce a complex pattern of rhythms
and a wide range of sounds, from
high, ringing notes near the edge to
deeper booms nearer the middle.

◁ GAMELAN

Xylophones are percussion instruments, because the bars are struck with hammers. On the Indonesian island of Bali, the gamelan orchestras consist almost entirely of xylophones of various sizes. They play rippling music of great complexity, accompanying temple dancing and ceremonies. The music is not written down; it is learned by heart and takes years of practice.

◁ THE MODERN DRUM KIT

Bands, such this one accompanying Jon Bon Jovi in New York, use a drum kit that was developed in the 20th century. It generally consists of a large base drum operated by a foot pedal, tom toms, a larger floor tom and a snare drum (or side drum), which has springlike metal snares underneath that produce a rattling sound. The kit includes a set of cymbals. The 'hi-hat' cymbal is operated by another foot pedal.

CASTANETS

Flamenco dancers in Spain add tension and excitement to their movements by making rapid clicking sounds with castanets held in the palm of their hands. Castanets consist of a pair of wooden shells hinged together, rather like a clam.

▷ XYLOPHONE

African xylophones, like this one from Burkina Faso, are often made of wooden bars. Hard woods give off a bright, ringing tone. The sound is amplified by sound boxes, or resonators, underneath the bars. In traditional African xylophones, the resonators are often made from dried gourds – pumpkin-like vegetables.

Wind instruments

THE simplest kind of wind instrument is a plain tube. When the player blows into it, the air inside vibrates and produces a sound. The sound can be varied by altering the pressure of the breath, or the length of the tube. The shorter the tube, or 'air column' the higher the note. Recorders and flutes have holes along the tube that alter the length of the tube when they are covered or uncovered. With trumpets, the valves alter the length of the tube. Wind instruments are divided into two main groups, woodwind and brass, according to the material from which they were originally made. Confusingly, though, some woodwind instruments, such as the flute saxophone, are made of metal – and even brass.

◪ THE FALL OF JERICHO

The trumpet is one of the oldest wind instruments. According to the Bible, the city of Jericho was defeated when the Israelites sounded their trumpets, causing the city walls to collapse. This would have taken place in about 1200 BC. The first trumpets (and horns) were plain tubes. A player adjusted the sound with lips and tongue.

◪ SOUSAPHONE

The bigger a wind instrument, the deeper the sound it will make. One of the biggest is the tuba, played in orchestras and brass bands to give a rich tone to the music. The sousaphone is a kind of tuba used in marching bands. It is named after the American composer of marching tunes John Sousa (1854–1932).

◩ LOUIS ARMSTRONG

Jazz music is often played on wind instruments. One of the most famous jazz musicians was the American Louis 'Satchmo' Armstrong (1900–71), a gifted trumpet player from New Orleans, the so-called 'birthplace of jazz'.

◩ REED INSTRUMENTS

Some woodwind instruments, such as the clarinet, have 'reeds'– thin strips of cane or metal that set up vibrations inside the instrument. A clarinet's reed is in the mouthpiece.

◪ SNAKE CHARMERS

In North Africa and Asia, some woodwind players are able to make highly poisonous cobras, a type of snake, rear their heads and sway in a kind of dance, as if 'charmed' by the music. In fact, cobras are almost deaf, and are really responding to vibrations in the ground and the swaying movement of the charmer's flute.

THE SERPENT

The serpent was a deep-sounding trumpet. It was used to play military and church music for about 400 years, until the 1800s. Its shape allowed the player to reach the holes far down the tube, which may be over 1.8 metres long.

◧ SCOTTISH BAGPIPES

Scottish bagpipes are woodwind instruments with a reed. Like a flute or a recorder, they have a tube with holes in, but instead of blowing directly into this, the player blows through another tube into a bag, where the air is stored. It is squeezed out again by the arm into the tube with holes – the 'chanter'. The bag also plays a continuous background sound through a set of drone pipes at the top of the instrument.

Stringed instruments

PLUCKING a taut rubber band produces a twanging sound, and the range of notes varies if the rubber band is stretched. This is also the principle of stringed instruments. Strings at various tensions are plucked, rubbed or struck to make them vibrate. A sound box amplifies the vibrations, making them louder. The shape of the sound box helps to improve the quality of the sound, making it richer and more rounded. Generally, the larger the sound box, the deeper and louder the sound.

◻ GREEK LYRE
The ancient Greeks played a harplike stringed instrument called a lyre, like the one shown on this Greek vase. But even older pictures show that lyres were used in Mesopotamia about 3000 BC. A lyre has two distinctive curved arms attached to a crossbar and a sound box.

◣ DULCIMER
The dulcimer has strings of different lengths stretched across a flat sound box. The player strikes the strings using a pair of flattened sticks, making a bright, ringing sound. Originating in the Middle East, the dulcimer was popular in Europe from the 1600s to the 1800s. The zither is similar, but its strings are plucked with the fingers.

◻ MARIACHI
A violin is played by drawing a bow across the four strings. In Mexico, groups of up to twelve musicians called mariachis play lively, popular songs on violins, guitars, double basses, harps and sometimes trumpets. They often play at weddings or simply in the street, where passers-by pay them a few dollars to play their favourite song.

◀ DOUBLE BASS

The giant of the violin family is the double bass. Its four thick strings can be plucked or played with a bow. The deep sounds are amplified by the huge wooden sound box. The double bass is played in orchestras and often forms part of jazz bands.

◢ SITAR OF INDIA

The great instrument of classical Indian music is the sitar. It has two sets of strings: one to play the melody, the other to set up a background vibration, giving the instrument its distinctive sound. The left hand presses, or 'stops' the strings to make different notes, while the right hand plucks them.

◣ JAPANESE KOTO

The koto is a kind of zither, played on the floor. The 13 silk strings are stretched over a wooden sound box measuring nearly 1.8 metres long. They are plucked with three plectrums, which are like nail extensions, worn on the right hand, while the left hand adjusts the notes. Each string is raised above the sound box on its own bridge, which can be moved to make different notes.

GUITAR

The guitar came to Europe in medieval times. It has had six strings since the 1600s. Different notes are made by pressing the strings over frets on the fingerboard, and strumming or plucking them with the other hand.

Keyboard instruments

COMPARED to percussion, wind and stringed instruments, keyboard instruments are a fairly recent invention, dating back only about a thousand years. Through a set of levers inside the instrument, each key can produce a precise note – all the player has to do is press the key. The kind of sound that results depends on the instrument. With a piano, the keys trigger hammers that strike a set of tuned strings. With an organ, the keys release air into a set of organ pipes, each sounding a different note. The advantage of keyboard instruments is that you can use all ten fingers (and even your feet) at the same time, and so produce a rich musical effect from a single instrument.

◢ CLAVICHORD

The clavichord was one of the first keyboard instruments. It was developed in the 1300s. Each key acted like a seesaw. When pressed, the other end rose up to hit one of the strings, which were arranged over a sound box, rather like a dulcimer.

◣ CHURCH ORGAN

The first keyboards were made for organs, but the keys were huge and had to be operated with a fist. Finger-sized keyboards were introduced in the 1300s. Keys, foot pedals, and knobs called 'stops' operate the flow of air into the organ pipes. Each pipe is tuned to one note. This church organ is in Naples, Italy.

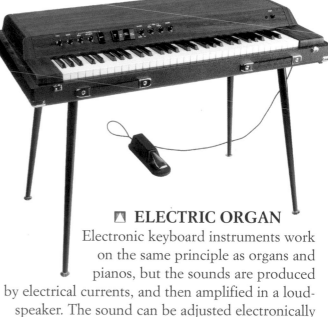

◢ ELECTRIC ORGAN

Electronic keyboard instruments work on the same principle as organs and pianos, but the sounds are produced by electrical currents, and then amplified in a loudspeaker. The sound can be adjusted electronically to make a very wide range of sounds, imitating all kinds of different instruments, including drums.

HARPSICHORD

While the earlier clavichord had to be set on a table, the harpsichord had its own legs. It developed after the 1500s through other similar instruments such as the virginal and spinet. The big difference with all these is that the strings are not struck, but plucked by a plectrum or 'jack' which is pushed past the string when a key is pressed. Harpsichords were very popular in the 18th century. Mozart learned to play the harpsichord as a child, astounding admiring audiences as he toured Europe from the age of six.

KEYBOARD SINGER

One advantage of the keyboard is that players can accompany themselves as they sing. This is why many songwriters – like the former Beatle Paul McCartney (b. 1942) – use the piano both to compose and to perform.

PLAYING THE PIANO

The full name of the piano is pianoforte, which means 'soft-loud' in Italian. It is so-called because it can be played loudly or softly, by altering pressure on the keys and by using the foot pedals. Invented in the early 1700s, the piano soon became more popular than the harpsichord, which gave players little opportunity to add 'expression' to their playing. Unlike the harpsichord, a piano's strings are not plucked, but struck with a 'hammer'. The metal strings are stretched across a massive metal frame, which may be set flat, as in a grand piano, or vertically, as in the more common upright piano. The hammers are operated by a system of levers attached to the keys.

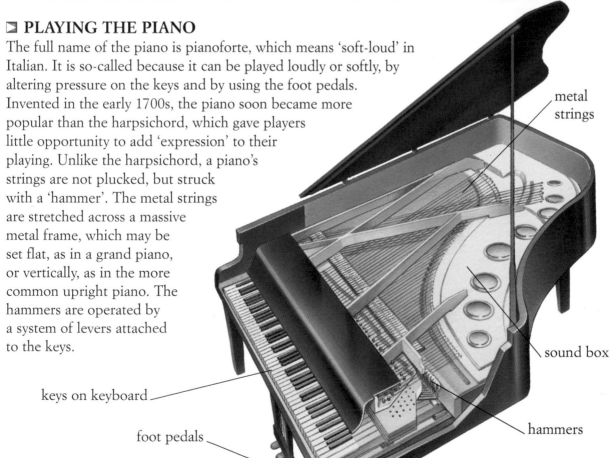

metal strings

sound box

keys on keyboard

hammers

foot pedals

Hybrid instruments

INSTRUMENTS are generally classed as belonging to one of three main categories: percussion, stringed, or wind. But some instruments, such as the saxophone, incorporate elements from more than one category (they are called hybrid instruments). Hybrids are the result of musicians and instrument makers trying to produce new kinds of sounds. Some inventions never really caught on, like the tromba marina, or 'sea trumpet' of the 17th century – a vast cello-like instrument whose one string produced a weird, trumpet-like sound.

For his opera *The Magic Flute* (1791), the German composer Mozart used a mechanical glockenspiel, a kind of keyboard-operated xylophone, the exact details of which have been lost.

◪ SAXOPHONE

One of the most popular wind instruments is the saxophone, or 'sax' which was invented in 1845. Although made of brass, it is classed as a woodwind instrument because it has a reed like a clarinet, and keys like an oboe or flute.

◪ ONDES MARTENOT

One of the earliest electronic instruments was invented in 1928 by the French inventor Maurice Martenot (1898–1980). It was also called an *ondes musicales*, meaning 'musical waves' in French. Played on a keyboard, the loudspeaker produces a great range of haunting sounds. Several major composers wrote music for it.

◪ ONE-MAN BAND

The ultimate hybrid instrument is a one man band. Using pedals, straps, and harnesses, a single musician can perform feats of great physical coordination, using hands, feet and mouth all at once to produce the sound of a mini-orchestra.

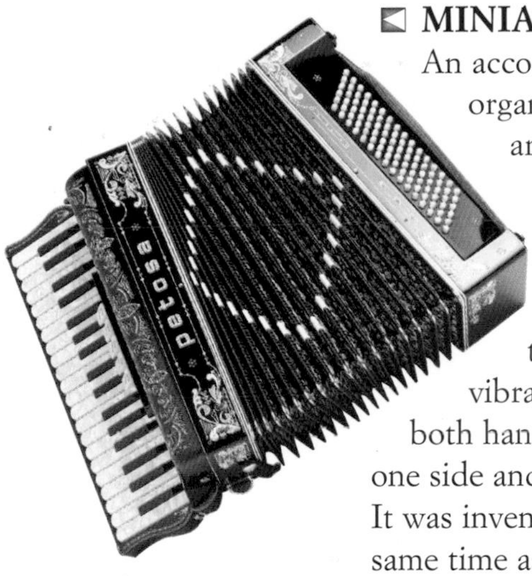

MINIATURE ORGAN

An accordion is a kind of miniature organ that can be carried around. With it strapped to the chest, a player uses both hands to stretch it open and squeeze it closed, forcing air past the reeds and making them vibrate. A tune is played using both hands, pressing the keys on one side and the buttons on the other. It was invented in 1822, about the same time as the concertina.

HURDY-GURDY

A hurdy-gurdy is a kind of mechanical violin. However, the strings are not played with a bow, but by a wheel turned with a handle. And instead of making notes by 'stopping' the strings on a fingerboard, the player presses the keys on a tiny keyboard set next to the strings. Both Mozart and Haydn wrote music for the hurdy-gurdy.

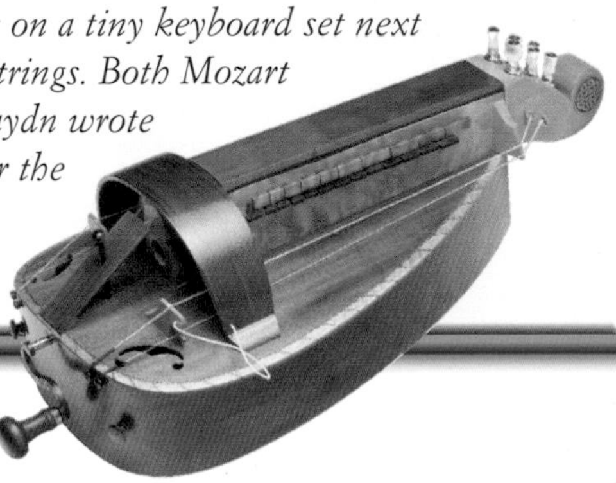

CARILLON BELLS

During medieval times, towns in the Netherlands, Belgium and Germany built towers with large bells in them to ring out the time and sound the alarm in the event of an emergency. The sets of bells became very elaborate, and had keyboards attached to them for playing tunes. This 20th-century carillon at the Zwinger Palace of Dresden, Germany, has a carillon of 40 bells made of the fine china called porcelain.

GLASS HARMONICA

If you run a wet finger around the rim of a glass, you may be able to produce a rather beautiful, eerie humming sound. This principle, and earlier instruments based on it, inspired the American statesman Benjamin Franklin (1706–90) to create the glass harmonica. It was popular for a time, and both Beethoven and Mozart wrote music for it.

Voice

THE simplest and most natural of all musical instruments is the human voice. We can assume that people have been singing since the beginning of human history. Pictures from the past, for example from ancient Egypt, are believed to show singers, but we can only guess what kind of sound they made. The human voice is like a musical instrument. The vocal cords set up vibrations, which are amplified in the chest, throat, mouth and nose. Professional singers have to have natural gifts such as an ability to sing in tune and with an attractive sound, but they may also need years of specialized training.

◤ SINGING TOGETHER

A number of people singing together in a choir can produce a rich sound, especially if the choir contains various types of voices, each singing a slightly different tune or 'part'. Choirs developed their skills in churches, but later began singing concerts, like this 18th-century Orphans' Choir in Venice.

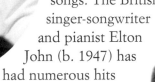

◀ ELTON JOHN

Singers are among the richest and most successful people in the modern music world— especially if they write their own songs. The British singer-songwriter and pianist Elton John (b. 1947) has had numerous hits since his first in 1970. His song "Candle in the Wind," sung at the funeral of Princess Diana, sold 35 million copies, making it an all-time top-selling single.

▶ THE THREE TENORS

In 1990, an operatic song, or aria, was chosen as the theme tune for the soccer World Cup. 'Nessun Dorma' from the opera *Turandot* by Giacomo Puccini (1858–1924), was sung by the three great tenors Placido Domingo, José Carreras and Luciano Pavarotti, and became a worldwide hit.

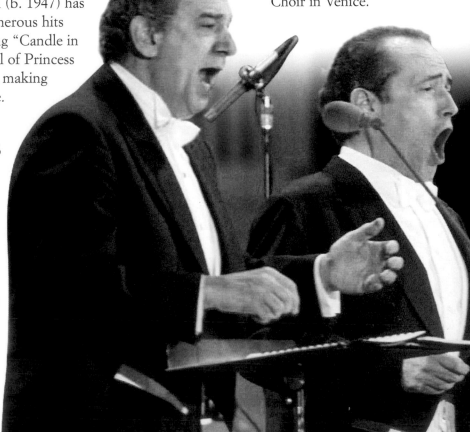

MUSICAL PLAYS

Singing is a central feature of musicals, a more popular kind of stage play than opera, in which all the words are sung.

Musicals often contain songs that become hits. One of the leading writers of musicals is Andrew Lloyd Webber (b. 1948). His musical *Cats* was first performed in 1981, and holds the record for the longest-running musical both in London and New York.

BALLAD SINGERS

Ballads are traditional songs that tell a story, often about the adventures of ordinary people. They were usually sung by one or two people, perhaps with guitars. Printed copies of the songs were often sold in the street.

SINGING AND TALKING

When African-American DJs in New York began half-singing, half-talking to dance music in the late 1970s, they launched 'rap'. Rap started as a rhyming commentary about daily life in the city, and the music was put together by 'sampling' excerpts of other records. Still popular, it is performed by current top American artists such as Ice T.

GOSPEL MUSIC

When African slaves in the United States converted to Christianity in the 19th century, they brought their own kind of rhythms to the hymns that they sang in church. A distinctive 'gospel music' developed – a joyful, energetic sound in praise of God, full of passion and emotion, and often accompanied by swaying and hand clapping.

Playing together

SINGLE – or solo – musicians can make an attractive sound on their own. But by playing with other musicians they can make a richer and more intricate sound. Groups of musicians have been playing together since the start of music, developing traditions and styles that have been passed down from one generation to the next. Most countries in the world have developed their own distinctive music. An Indonesian gamelan orchestra, for example, is utterly different from a Western chamber orchestra, and its music is just as complex.

◪ EGYPTIAN MUSIC

In the tomb of a royal scribe in ancient Egypt, wall paintings from about 1360 BC show a group of musicians playing for dancers. Such groups may have included pipes, flutes, harps and drums. Dancers sometimes played tambourines.

◁ GREAT COMPOSER

In the past, dancers at balls were accompanied by orchestras like this one. One of the greatest composers of dance music was the Austrian Johann Strauss (1825–99), who wrote a large number of famous waltzes, including 'The Blue Danube'.

◻ ORCHESTRA

Since the 19th century, large-scale classical music has been played by symphony orchestras with about 100 musicians. To make a balanced sound, the musicians are grouped in sections, usually with the strings at the front, woodwind and then brass behind, and percussion at the back. Composers can choose to use more or fewer musicians, or add instruments such as harps.

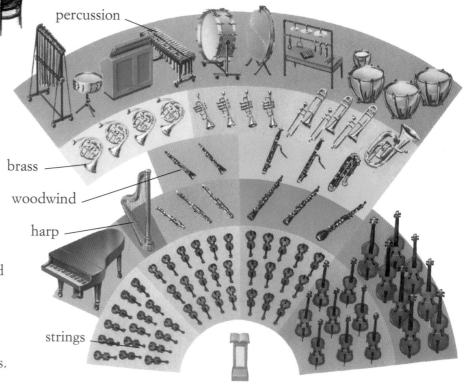

percussion

brass

woodwind

harp

strings

CONDUCTOR

The job of the conductor is to rehearse and direct the musicians. He or she shows them the speed and rhythm (often using a baton), and how to obtain the right balance in sound.

◄ JAZZ BAND

The exciting rhythms of jazz became hugely popular in the 1920s. Joe 'King' Oliver and his Creole Jazz Band, from Chicago, formed one of the most famous groups. Jazz bands of the time often included drums, strings and a piano.

◄ FOLK BAND

Folk dance music is usually played by small bands of about five or so players, as with this band in Lithuania. They play traditional tunes, dating back perhaps hundreds of years. The type of music that they play, as well as the traditional costumes of the dancers, is often closely associated with national identity.

◄ MARCHING BAND

Soldiers marching to war were often accompanied by bands that played tunes to lift their spirits and help them to march in step. The bands consisted entirely of wind and percussion instruments. Most modern marching bands have nothing to do with the army, but they use the same kinds of instruments and wear uniforms.

Composers

ALL music has to be created, or composed, by someone. A large proportion of traditional music was created hundreds of years ago by unknown composers, and passed down from one generation to the next, being altered and perhaps improved at each stage. In Europe, composers developed the practice of writing down music. As a result, we know the names of the composers, and also more or less how they wanted the music to sound. Many Western composers developed the ability to write complex music straight onto the page by first imagining the sounds in their heads. They could then give the music to an orchestra to play.

◤ WRITTEN MUSIC
In medieval times, composers devised a kind of visual picture of sounds, so that they could be read by others. It was based on the musical scale – the progression of notes from lowest to highest, as played on an instrument. Each note in the scale was given a position on a set of horizontal lines. By reading the written music from left to right, musicians could see the order in which to play the notes.

◄ MONTEVERDI
The Italian composer Claudio Monteverdi (1567–1643) became famous for his church music. He also wrote one of the first operas, *Orfeo,* in 1607. Although Monteverdi lived and worked in and around Venice, his fame spread because he was able to publish his work in printed form.

◲ COMPOSING MUSIC
When creating a complicated piece of work for many instruments, composers often try out their ideas on a piano. One of the greatest-ever composers, the German Ludwig van Beethoven (1770–1827), worked in this way. In sketch books, he wrote down the music that he wanted each instrument to play, before taking it to the orchestra to try out.

◀ THE SCORE – PRINTED MUSIC

The written or printed music that an orchestra plays from is called the 'score'. It shows all the parts that the different instruments play and how they fit together. This is part of the handwritten score of the opera *The Barber of Seville* by the Italian composer Gioachino Rossini (1782–1868).

◀ YOUNG COMPOSER

Wolfgang Amadeus Mozart (1756–91) was one of the greatest composers of Western music. Born and brought up in Austria, he was a child prodigy who began composing at the age of five, and went on to write church music, concertos, symphonies, and operas. He composed entire works in his head and wrote them straight onto the page. Mozart led a very full life in Salzburg and Vienna, and died aged just 35.

MUSICAL NOTES

Written notes (or notation) do not simply show their 'pitch' – how high and low they are. They also show how long they should be played for. Notes range in length from a whole note (or semi-breve) which is played for four beats, to a sixteenth note (or semi-quaver), which lasts for a quarter of a beat.

whole note   quarter note

half note   eighth note

sixteenth note

◀ COMPUTER COMPOSITION

Max Mathews was a pioneer of computer music. In 1963 he helped to devise a way of 'synthesizing' musical sounds into a digital form that could be stored in a computer and played back. Computers can store vast quantities of sound information, and so can imitate all kinds of instruments, and even styles of playing them.

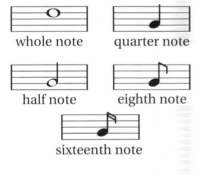

Classical music

WESTERN classical music grew first out of church music. The search for an ever more complex and rich sound led to improved standards of instrument making. This would not have been possible without patrons – rich people who paid composers to write new music, and paid musicians to perform it. During the 15th century, kings and nobles also became important patrons of fine music. Classical music developed further because composers could write down their music, and then have it printed – so orchestras anywhere could play it, even if the composer was not present. Orchestras try to play the music accurately, but also to 'interpret' it, giving it their own individual character and feeling.

◤ BEETHOVEN
Ludwig van Beethoven (1720–1827) was the most brilliant pianist of his day. He played with great passion – a passion that is also found in his many compositions. The traditional orchestra had to be enlarged to play his complex symphonies, which were considered extremely modern at the time.

◁ SCHOENBERG
The Austrian composer Arnold Schoenberg (1874–1951) was a pioneer of modern music. He abandoned the traditional harmonies of the eight-note scale, and instead worked with all the notes, producing an entirely new sound called 'atonal music'.

◁ OPERA
Opera began as a kind of musical entertainment, combining music, singing and dance. Gradually it developed into the form it has today, a full play in which the entire story is sung to classical music. Shown here is a performance of *Aida*, a tragic story set in ancient Egypt, by the great opera composer Giuseppe Verdi (1813–1901).

◱ BALLET

Classical music has been written specially for ballet. *Swan Lake,* for example – for which this is a costume – was written by the great Russian composer Pyott Ilíyich Tchaikovsky (1840–93). It was first performed at the Bolshoi Theatre in Moscow in 1877. Tchaikovsky also wrote the music for operas and symphonies.

◱ HANDEL

George Frideric Handel (1685– 1759) was a German composer and a gifted musician, playing violin and harpsichord. He came to England in 1712 and worked for Queen Anne and King George I. One of his most popular works is *Music for the Royal Fireworks,* designed to be played outdoors with a firework display.

STRAVINSKY

Some of the most exciting ballet of the 20th century was performed by the Russian company the Ballets Russes, led by Sergei Diaghilev. He commissioned a number of composers to create music for them. One of these was Igor Stravinsky (1882–1971), who wrote Firebird, Petrushka *and* The Rite of Spring, *and became one of the greatest composers of the 20th century.*

◱ CLASSICAL MUSIC TODAY

A few years ago, many people thought that classical music had lost its popular appeal. But with the help of CDs, TV exposure and classical music radio stations, a new generation of talented and glamorous performers like Vanessa Mae (b. 1979) have found a new audience, and demonstrated that classical music is very much alive.

Improvisation

SOME kinds of music are not bound to a written score. Instead, the musicians are free to play what they like and express their own emotions, although they usually start and end with a recognizable theme. This kind is called 'improvisation'. It is most closely associated with jazz music. In a famous piece of jazz, for instance, the American saxophonist John Coltrane played his own highly original version of 'My Favourite Things' from the popular musical *The Sound of Music*. But many other kinds of music also involve improvisation, such as blues, rock, Indian sitar music and traditional dance music.

◪ STÉPHANE GRAPPELLI

The French jazz musician Stéphane Grappelli (1908–97) played the violin in an utterly original way, at great speed and with a highly individual style of improvisation. In the 1930s he played with the great jazz guitarist Django Reinhardt (1910–53).

◪ PLAYING THE SAXOPHONE

John Coltrane (1926–67) was one of the greatest American jazz musicians. He played tenor saxophone with some of the top bands of his day, such those led by Dizzie Gillespie (1917–93) and Miles Davis (1926–91), before forming his own quartet. His innovative music laid many of the foundations of modern jazz.

◪ ELVIS PRESLEY

In the 1950s, young white American musicians started to produce upbeat guitar music based on 'country-and-western' and black 'rhythm and blues'. It was called 'rock 'n' roll' and the 'King' was Elvis Presley (1935–77). At first he was thought of as a rebel, but he went on to sing many songs that have become classic hits.

◁ DIXIELAND, SWING AND BEBOP

Jazz developed in New Orleans in about 1900. 'Dixieland' jazz created a fun, raucous sound based on popular songs. In the 1930s and 1940s jazz musicians in big bands created the smoother, plusher dance sound of 'swing'. The faster, more rhythmic 'bebop' jazz was introduced by smaller groups in the late 1940s. One of the key musicians in this movement was the alto sax player Charlie 'Bird' Parker (1920–55), seen on the right here playing in New York in 1949.

▷ ROCK MUSIC

In the late 1960s, bands started to mix rock 'n' roll, jazz and blues, amplified it electronically and created the style now known as 'rock'. The Irish group U2 emerged as one of the leading rock bands in the 1980s, fronted by the singer Bono (Paul Hewson, b. 1960). U2 was hugely popular in both Britain and America.

WURLITZER ORGAN

Before 1927, movies had no soundtrack. Instead the 'silent movies' were accompanied by musicians who watched the film and made up music to mirror the action. In 1911 a US organ-making company called Wurlitzer began producing elaborate cinema organs that could make a wide range of orchestral sounds and sound effects.

◩ RHYTHM AND BLUES

The blues is a type of heartfelt folk music that was originally sung by African slaves in the southern states of America. It has played a key role in the development of modern popular music. In the 1940s it reached a wider audience through a fusion with jazz, called 'rhythm and blues' (or R & B). One of the best-known R & B musicians was the guitarist B. B. King (b. 1925), a great promoter of the blues.

Recorded music

THE development of sound-recording devices has transformed the way we listen to music. Before the invention of the first gramophones, the only way to hear music was to see it played live – or to play it oneself. But gramophones made it possible to hear top performers and music from other parts of the world, without leaving home. The spread of radio in the 1920s had a similar effect. Today, most of the music we listen to is recorded music. With digital technology the quality of recorded music has become exceptionally good – better, often, than live music. But many people argue that live performances still convey more of a sense of inspiration and emotion than recorded music ever can.

◣ SOUND RECORDING

The first gramophone, called a phonograph, was produced by the American inventor Thomas Alva Edison in 1878. It used cylinders to record and play sounds. Ten years later the first flat disc was introduced. A needle picked up the sound from grooves in the disc.

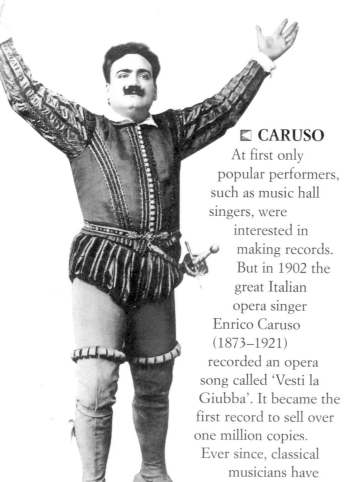

◣ CARUSO

At first only popular performers, such as music hall singers, were interested in making records. But in 1902 the great Italian opera singer Enrico Caruso (1873–1921) recorded an opera song called 'Vesti la Giubba'. It became the first record to sell over one million copies. Ever since, classical musicians have made recordings.

◣ RADIO ENTERTAINMENT

The radio was invented by the Italian Guglielmo Marconi in 1894. At first it was designed only to transmit simple messages, but in 1906 music was broadcast. By the time this picture was taken in the 1940s, many households in Europe and America had a radio. It was the most popular form of family entertainment before the arrival of television in the 1950s.

◁ RECORDING STUDIO

In a modern recording studio, electronic equipment records sounds on a number of tracks, often one instrument at a time. The sound engineers can alter the tracks, by changing the pitch, for example, or adding new sounds. Then they 'mix' all the tracks together and carefully adjust the balance between the tracks to produce a finished recording.

▽ QUEEN OF POP

Ever since her hit single 'Holiday' in 1984, the American singer and songwriter Madonna (Madonna Louise Ciccone, b. 1958) has been a top recording artist. She has had 35 top-ten hits, and 50 of her records have sold over a million copies. A master of publicity, she continually alters her image through her pop videos.

▷ JUKE BOX

In the days when records were produced on plastic or vinyl discs (from the late 1940s to the 1990s), they came in two forms: LPs (long-playing) and 45s (smaller records that revolved faster, at 45 revolutions per minute). The top-ten charts were based entirely on 'singles' which came on 45s. In places like bars, cafés and youth clubs, a selection of 45s was put into a machine called a juke box. Listeners put money in the slot, selected the record they wanted to hear, and the machine played it for them.

CD

The trouble with vinyl discs was that they could be easily damaged by scratching. In the 1990s a new kind of record began to replace vinyl. Compact discs (CDs) were not only neater and more solid: their digital and laser technology offered a more accurate recording, and a better sound quality.

The music industry

IN the days before recorded music, composers, and music publishers made money by printing and selling sheet music. Now, with CDs, cassettes, pop videos, and more recently the Internet, music publishing has become a multi-million-dollar international industry. The top stars of popular music sell millions of copies of their recordings all over the world, and because they earn a percentage of the sale price as a 'royalty', they can earn vast sums of money. There is considerable skill in spotting, promoting and nurturing talent. In the pop music business, musical talent may be less important than youth and personality. But classical music still demands very high standards of musicianship.

◢ CLASSICAL STAR

One of the most fascinating stars of classical music was the Italian violinist and composer Niccolo Paganini (1782–1840). He was a 'virtuoso' – a player with dazzling gifts – who could play extremely complex pieces, and at such great speed that some people suggested he must be in league with the Devil.

◤ PAUL ROBESON

Many people came to know the American Paul Robeson (1898–1976) through his recorded music, and he became one of the most important black singers of his time, famous for his rich, bass voice. Robeson was a theatre and screen actor as well as a singer. He first made his name internationally in a tour of the stage musical *Show Boat* in 1928, in which he sang his best-known song 'Ol' Man River'.

◥ MUSIC SHOP

Since the early history of music, instrument makers have played a vital role in the music business. The better the quality of an instrument, the better the sound it makes, and usually the more it costs. Good music shops offer a wide selection of instruments for players to try out.

◀ SPICE WORLD

A feature of modern pop music is the girl band or boy band. Producers in the music industry select a group of young and glamorous singers, find suitable songs for them, and then launch them in a blaze of publicity. The Spice Girls were an immediate success in 1996, and had number-one hits with their first three singles.

THE BEATLES

The world's most successful recording group of the 1960s was the British band the Beatles. The 'Fab Four' were Paul McCartney (b. 1942), John Lennon (1940–80), George Harrison (1943–2002), and Ringo Starr (b. 1940).

▶ INVENTIVE SONGWRITER

In the late 1960s, there was a sharp division between pop and rock music. People tended to like one and hate the other. During the early 1970s, the gap was closed by inventive songwriters like British singer David Bowie (b. 1947), who was also famous for his extravagant stage performances.

☑ HUGE SUCCESS

One of the most successful 'boy bands'w of the 1990s was the American group the Backstreet Boys. All talented singers, they formed in 1992 and became stars first in Europe and Canada. Their breakthrough at home came in 1997 with their album Backstreet Boys, which sold 13 million copies.

World music

LIKE many other industries, the music business has become global. One advantage of this is that all kinds of musical styles from around the world are now being recorded, listened to and studied. Such styles range from traditional music, whose patterns have not changed for hundreds of years, to modern hybrid forms of music – a blend of local traditional music with modern electronic pop. Popular music today may show influences of South American dance music, North African singing, Indian tabla rhythms, or Indonesian gamelan. Music is always changing and developing, and today the mix is becoming richer and more complex than ever.

◪ INUIT DRUM DANCE

The Inuit of Canada and Greenland perform a traditional dance to the beat of a large, caribou-skin drum (a *qilaut*). Individual men take turns to play the drum and dance, accompanied by singing. The dances often act out a story, told in the singing, usually about hunting or animals.

◪ SOUTH AFRICAN SINGER

Black South Africa has a rich tradition in music. One of the first singers to demonstrate this to the world was Miriam Makeba (b. 1932), who moved to the United States in the 1960s to escape the harsh apartheid regime. Combining music with political activities, she recorded many Xhosa and Zulu songs. She returned to South Africa in 1990.

◪ MUSIC FOR THE WORLD

An important development in the promotion of world music was the creation of WOMAD (World of Music, Arts and Dance), which held its first festival in 1982. Since then there have been more than 90 festivals and events in 20 countries, featuring musicians from all over the world.

◁ INDIAN FOLK MUSIC

Bhangra is the name of a type of folk dance in Punjab, a region bordering north India and Pakistan. This acrobatic and colourful dance is performed to celebrate the harvest. In the 1980s, the Asian community in Britain developed a modern dance music with the same name, blending traditional Indian music with electronic instruments, drum machines, reggae and disco music.

◁ PAUL SIMON—SINGER-SONGWRITER

The American singer-songwriter Paul Simon (b. 1941) became famous in the 1960s and 1970s as half of the duo Simon and Garfunkel (with Art Garfunkel, b. 1941). In 1986 he worked with musicians from the South African townships, such as the Ladysmith Black Mambazo, to produce Graceland, a hugely successful record album and tour. He continues to explore the fusion between Western, African, and South American music.

☑ REGGAE MUSIC

Reggae is a type of dance music from Jamaica, noted for its use of a heavy, offbeat rhythm. It was made world-famous in the 1970s by Bob Marley (1945–81) and his group The Wailers. After 'No Woman, No Cry' (1975), he had a string of hits, until his early death from cancer. Reggae was one of the first non-American music styles to have a major impact on pop music.

RAVI SHANKAR

'The Godfather of World Music' is how the great Indian sitar player Ravi Shankar (b. 1920) has been described. He has been playing his music around the world since 1954. Not only is he a supreme performer of Indian classical music, but he has also studied ways of mixing it with Western classical music.

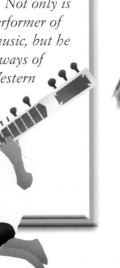

Glossary

AMPLIFY
To make louder. Sounds can be amplified by sound boxes or resonators, or electronically by turning them into electrical signals using a microphone, and passing the signals through an electronic amplifier into loudspeakers.

APARTHEID
The policy once held by the South African government that kept black people separate from white people, and gave them fewer human rights, to keep white people in power.

ATONAL MUSIC
A form of modern music composition where the notes or sounds are not arranged in the traditional order of scales and harmonies, but in a more abstract way.

BALL
A very grand and formal social occasion, where there is space for people to dance to a band or group of musicians.

BAMBOO
Tall, tree-like types of grass that grow in tropical countries. The woody stems are hollow and have many uses, from musical pipes to scaffolding poles.

BASS
The very low sounds or musical notes, played by large instruments such as a double bass or a tuba, or sung by a man with a very deep voice.

BATON
A stick waved by the conductor of an orchestra to emphasise the rhythm and pattern of the music, so that everyone plays or sings the notes in the correct way at the correct time.

BRASS
A shiny, yellowish metal which is an alloy, or mixture, of the pure metals copper and zinc. It is used to make wind instruments such as cornets, trumpets, trombones and horns, which form the brass section of an orchestra.

CHANTER
The pipe on a set of bagpipes which has holes along it, which are covered with the fingers, so that a tune is played when the bag squeezes air through it.

CONCERTINA
A small version of an accordion, usually with a six-sided bellows-type bag that pushes air over reeds and makes them vibrate to produce notes. The notes are controlled by a keyboard.

CYMBALS
Percussion instruments which consist of thin concave metal plates, like shallow dishes. They can be played by striking them with a stick, or by clapping two of them together to make a crashing sound.

DIGITAL
Digital sound is recorded, not as continuous up-and-down waves, but as codes of numbers or digits, which usually results in a clearer, purer, more accurate recording.

DJ
Disc jockey, a person who chooses and plays music from vinyl records, compact discs or tapes, on the radio or television, or at dances, discos or nightclubs.

DRONE PIPES
The pipes within a set of bagpipes which play continuous, unchanging background sounds, as air is blown through them from the bag.

FLAMENCO
A style of mainly Spanish singing, dancing and playing, usually accompanied by the guitar. The dancers stamp their feet and click wooden castanets in their hands while they move gracefully and proudly.

FOLK DANCE
The traditional dance of a group of people or a particular country. Its movements and steps are passed down from generation to generation, and quite often performed in traditional costume.

FRETS
The series of small metal bars found on a fingerboard or fretboard of a stringed instrument, such as a guitar. When a string is pressed down onto a fret and made to vibrate, a certain note is played.

HIT
A song or a type of recording that is extremely popular, often selling many copies so that it enters the best-seller charts or 'hit parade'.

HYBRID
A cross-breed or a mixture – or in music, an instrument which falls into more than one of the traditional categories. For example, the saxophone is seen as both a brass instrument, such as a trumpet, and also a woodwind instrument, because it has a vibrating reed just like the clarinet.

JAZZ
A form of popular music, originating from African Americans, often with a fast or syncopated rhythm, complicated musical pattern and tunes, and improvised words. (made up at the time).

LASER
A special high-energy light of a single pure colour. Lasers can be controlled very precisely and are used to shine at the microscopic pit-like marks on the surface of a compact disc, which hold all the digital codes for the sound.

LEVERS
Special bars which have an anchor, or fulcrum, usually near the middle, so that each end can move like a see-saw. A piano key is a kind of lever, and when one end is pushed down by the player, the other end swings up and strikes a string.

MEDIEVAL
Usually referring to the Middle or Dark Ages, a 1000-year period in history, which generally began at the end of the Roman era, around 400 AD, and ended with the Renaissance period, around 1400 AD.

MELODY
A sequence of musical notes, up and down the scales, which produces a recognizable and usually pleasant tune.

PATRON
A rich person, or benefactor, who pays, or gives gifts to, or who otherwise assists a poorer but talented person such as a musician, artist, composer or actor.

PIONEER
Someone who does things that no one else has done before, such as exploring unknown lands, or developing new musical styles and playing techniques.

PLECTRUM
A device for plucking the strings of a musical instrument, especially a guitar, such as a small triangular piece of plastic held between thumb and finger, or a ring of plastic worn on the end of the finger with a flap like an extended fingernail.

PRODIGY
A person with unusual or exceptional talents, especially a child or young person who shows abilities which are far greater than usual for his or her age.

QUARTET
Any group of four. In music, the term usually refers to a group of singers, or musicians who play instruments from the same category such as a string quartet.

REHEARSE
To prepare for a public performance, such as playing a piece of music or acting in a play, by practising over and over again.

RESONATE
When the vibrations of a sound produce further vibrations in nearby objects or air spaces, which enhance or amplify (make louder) the original sound.

ROYALTY
In music, a type of payment. When a work such as a book, play, invention or piece of music makes money, the creator of that work is paid a proportion of the money, called a royalty.

SCRIBE
A person who writes. Long ago, when few people could write and there was no printing, scribes copied out important documents and books.

STOPS
The knobs on an organ that allow the player to regulate the tone, by moving sliders that open or close sets or ranks of pipes.

STRUM
To sweep the thumb, fingers or a plectrum up and/or down across strings, especially on a guitar, to produce musical notes or groups of notes called chords.

SYNTHESIZE
To make artificially or put together from various sources.

In music, the synthesizer is a machine that can make a huge variety of sounds electronically, which can resemble other instruments and even produce sound effects such as the wind or thunder.

UNIFORM
Anything that stays the same, such as the identical clothes worn by people who belong to the same group or organization, such as a school, an army or a musical band.

VALVE
A device for controlling the passage of air or fluid through a pipe. (A water tap is a type of valve.) In a brass instrument, the valves alter the effective length of the tube and therefore the note played.

VIBRATIONS
Regular, repeated, often rapid movements, to and fro. Musical instruments work by vibrating particles or molecules in the air, which are called sound waves and pass through the air to the ears.

VOCAL CORDS
Fibrous folds in the lining of the voice box, or larynx, in the lower throat. Sounds of the voice are produced by tightening the cords and blowing air over them from the lungs, so that they vibrate.

WALTZ
A dance performed by two people who hold each other and twirl around by moving their feet in a sequence of steps, with a rhythm in groups of three beats.

ZITHER
A musical instrument consisting of a wooden sound box, over which strings are stretched. The instrument rests on a table or the players knees while the strings are plucked.

Index

A

Aborigines 9
accordion 19
African music 21, 29, 35
Aida 26
alto saxophone 29
American music 21, 29
aria 20
Armstrong, Louis *13*
Asia, music 13, 35
atonal music 26
Austria, music 25
Aztec drums *10*

B

Backstreet Boys 33
bagpipes 13
Bali, music 11
ballads 21
ballet 27
Ballets Russes 27
bands 28, 33
    brass 12
    drums 11
    folk 23
    jazz 23
    marching 23
bass drum 11
baton 23
Beatles, The 17, *33*
bebop 29
Beethoven, Ludwig van
    19, 24, 26
Belgium, music 19
bells 10, 19
bhangra 35
Bible music 12
big bands 29
blues 28, 29
Bolshoi Theatre 27
Bon Jovi, Jon *11*
Bono 29
bow 14, 15
bow harps 8
Bowie, David *33*
boy bands 33
brass bands 12
brass instruments 12,
    18, 22
Britain, music 29, 35
Burkino Faso, music 11

C

Canada, music 33, 34
carillon bells *19*
Carreras, José 20
Caruso, Enrico *30*

cassettes 32
castanets 11
Cats 21
CDs 27, 31, 32
Central American music
    9
chamber orchestra 22
choir 20
Christianity, music 21
church music 13, 16, 20,
    21, 24, 25, 26
cinema 29
clarinet 13
classical music 22,
    26–27, 30, 32, 35
clavichord *16*, 17
Coltrane, John 29
composers 18, 22,
    24–25, 26, 27, 32
composing 17
computer music 25
concertina 19
concertos 25
concerts 20
conductors 23
country-and-western 28
Creole Jazz Band 23
cymbals 10, 11

D

dance 9, 22, 23, 28, 29,
    34, 35
    Egyptian 8
    flamenco 11
    Davis, Miles 28
Diaghilev, Sergei 27
didgeridoo *9*
digital music 25, 30, 31
disco music 35
discs 30, 31
DJs 11, 21
Domingo, Placido 20
double bass 14, 15
drone pipes 13
drum machines 35
drums 10, 11, 22, 23, 34
    early 8
    electric organ 16
dulcimer 14, 16

E

Edison, Thomas Alva *30*
Egyptian music 8, 20,
    22, 26
eight-note scale 26
electric organ *16*
electronic music 16, 31,

34, 35
England, music 27
Europe, music 8, 14, 15,
    17, 24, 33

F

Firebird Petruska 27
flamenco dancers 11
floor-tom 11
flute saxophone 12
flutes 10, 12, 13, 22
folk music 23, 29, 35
Franklin, Benjamin 19
frets 15

G

Gabriel, Peter 34
Gambia, music 10
gamelan music 11, 22,
    34
Garfunkel, Art 35
Genesis 34
Germany, music 19
Gillespie, Dizzie 28
girl bands 33
glass harmonica 19
global music **34–35**
glokenspiel 18
gongs 10
Gospel music *21*
gramophones 30
grand piano 17
Grappelli, Stéphane 28
Greeks, music 9, 14
Greenland, music 34
groups 33
guitars 14, 15, 21, 28

H

hammers,
    percussion
    instruments 11
    piano 16, 17
Handel, George Frideric
    27
harmonica, glass 19
harmonies 26
harps 8, 14, 22
harpsichord 17, 27
Harrison, George 33
Haydn 19
Hewson, Paul 29
horns 12
hurdy-gurdy 19
hybrid instruments
    18–19
hymns 21

I

Ice T Rapper *21*
improvisation **28–29**
Indian music 15, 28, 34,
    35
Indonesian music 11,
    22, 34
Inuit music *34*
Italian music 16, 17, 24

J/K

Jamaican music 35
Japan, music 10, 15
jazz 13, 15, 23, 28, 29
John, Elton *20*
juke box *31*
keyboard instruments
    16–17, 18, 19
King, B. B. 29
koto *15*

L

Ladysmith Black
    Mambazo 35
Lennon, John 33
Lithuania, folk band 23
Lloyd Webber, Andrew
    21
log drums 10
loudspeaker 16, 18
lyre 14

M

Madonna 31
Mae, Vanessa *27*
Makeba, Miriam 34
mariachis 14
Marley, Bob 35
Martenot, Maurice 18
Mathews, Max 25
Mayan music 9
McCartney, Paul 17, 33
medieval music 8, 15,
    19, 24
melody 15
Mesopotamia, music 14
Mexico, music 9, 10, 14
Middle East, music 14
military music 13
modern music 26, 34, 35
Monteverdi, Claudio 24
Moscow, ballet 27
Mozart, Wolfgang
    Amadeus 17, 18, 19,
    25
music,
    classical **26–27**

composers **24–25**
earliest **8–9**
Egyptian 22
global 34, 35
improvised **28–29**
recorded **30–31**
Music for the Royal Fireworks 27
music hall singers 30
music industry **32–33**, 34
musical instruments, earliest 8-9
hybrid 18-19
keyboard 16-17
percussion 10-11
stringed 14-15
wind 12-13
musicals 21, 32
musicians 18, 26
groups **22–23**

N
Nazca drum 8
Netherlands, music 19
New Orleans jazz 13, 29
North African music 13, 34
notation *25*
notes 26
drums 10
keyboards 16
panpipes 9
stringed instruments 14
wind instruments 12
written 24, 25

O
Oliver, Joe 23
ondes martenot *18*
one-man band *18*
opera 18, 20, 24, 25, 26, 27, 30
orchestras 22, 24, 25, 26
brass instruments 12, 22
gamelan 11
strings 15, 22
Orfeo 24
organ 16, 29
Orphans Choir, Venice *20*

P/Q
Paganini, Nicolú 32
Pakistan music 35

panpipes 9
Parker, Charlie 29
patrons 26
Pavarotti, Luciano *20*
percussion instruments **10–11**, 18, 22, 23
Peru, music 8
phonograph 30
pianist 20, 26
piano 16, *17*, 23, 24
pianoforte 17
pipes 16, 22
pitch 25, 31
plectrums 15, 17
pop music 31, 32, 33, 34, 35
pop-videos 31, 32
popular music 29, 32, 34
Presley, Elvis 28
printed music 24, 25, 26, 32
Puccini, Giacomo 20
quartet 28

R
radio 27, 30
rap music 21
record album 33, 35
recorded music **30–31**, 32, 34
recorders 12, 13
recording studio *31*
records 21
reeds 9, 13, 18, 19
reggae 35
Reinhardt, Django 28
religious ceremonies 8, 10
resonation 10, 11
rhythm 10, 21, 23, 34, 35
rhythm and blues 28, 29
Robeson, Paul 32
rock music 28, 29, 33
rock 'n roll 28, 29
Rossini, Gioachino 25
Russian ballet 27

S
Salzburg, music 25
saxophone 18, 28, 29
scale 10, 24, 26
Schoenberg, Arnold 26
score *25*, 28
Scotland, bagpipes 13
Shankar, Ravi *35*
sheet music 32
Shinto temple drums *10*

Show Boat 32
silent movies 29
Simon, Paul *35*
singer-songwriters 20, 35
singing 9, 20-21, 30, 32, 34
Egyptian 8
keyboards 17
opera 26
sirens, drums 10
sitar 15, 28, 35
skin, drums 10
slave music 21, 29
snake charmers *13*
snare drum 11
solo musicians 22
songwriting 17, 20, 33, 35
sound 9, 20
hybrid instruments 18
percussion instruments 10
stringed instruments 14
wind instruments 12
sound box 11
keyboards 16
piano 17
strings 14, 15
sound effects 29
sound recording 30
sound track 29
Sousa, John 12
sousaphone *12*
South African music 34, 35
South American music 8, 34, 35
Spain, music 11
Spice Girls *33*
spinet 17
Starr, Ringo *33*
steel drums 10
stops, organ 16
Strauss, Johann 22
Stravinsky, Igor 27
stringed instruments 8, **14–15**, 23
early 8
orchestra 22
Swan Lake 27
swing 29
symphonies 25, 26, 27
symphony orchestras 22
synthesized music 25

T/U
tabla music 34
tambourine *8*, 22
Tchaikovsky, Pyott Ilíyich 27
temple music 9, 10, 11
tenor saxophone 28
The Barber of Seville 25
The Magic Flute 18
The Rite of Spring 27
The Sound of Music 28
Three Tenors *20*
tom-toms 11
Trinidad, steel drums 10
tromba marina 18
trumpets 12, 13, 14
tuba 12
Turandot 20
U2 *29*
United States, music 21, 23, 33

V
Verdi, Giuseppe 26
vibration 12, 13
reeds 19
strings 14, 15
vocal cords 20
Vienna, music 25
violin 14, 15, 27, 28, 32
virtuoso 32
vocal cords 9, 20
voice 9, 10, **20–21**, 32

W/X/Z
wadaiko drums 10
waltzes 22
Western music 35
chamber orchestra 22
classical 26
composers 24, 25
whistle 9
wind instruments **12–13**, 18, 23
WOMAD 34
woodwind instruments 12, 13, 22
world music **34–35**
written music 24, 25, 26, 28
Wurlitzer organ 29
Xhosa music 34
xylophones 10, *11*, 18
zither 14, 15
Zulu music 34